MOST-US[ED WORD]S
AND PHRASES

Diamond Jubilee Series

John Robert Gregg

Louis A. Leslie

Charles E. Zoubek

Shorthand written by Charles Rader

GREGG

75

GREGG DIVISION
McGRAW-HILL BOOK COMPANY
New York   Chicago   Dallas   San Francisco
Toronto   London   Sydney

MOST-USED WORDS AND PHRASES, DIAMOND JUBILEE SERIES

9 10 11 12 WC WC 76 75 74 73 72

24592

Library of Congress Catalog Card No. 61-18133

Preface

Most-Used Words and Phrases, Diamond Jubilee Series, is a compilation of 3,822 words and 1,569 phrases classified according to the lessons of *Gregg Shorthand, Diamond Jubilee Series.* Each word and phrase, together with its shorthand outline, is listed according to the lesson and the principle of *Gregg Shorthand, Diamond Jubilee Series,* under which it can first be written.

Selection of Words

The words were taken from the first 10,000 words in order of frequency as indicated in the Horn-Peterson *Basic Vocabulary of Business Letters,* which contains 14,834 different words found in a count of 1,500,000 words of business letters chosen from 26 kinds of businesses. The words selected for inclusion in the lists of *Most-Used Words and Phrases* are those that are of the greatest usefulness to the stenographer in the business office.

Many of the first 10,000 words in order of frequency in the Horn-Peterson study are simple derivatives in *-ing,* *-s,* and *-ed;* and the student can easily form shorthand outlines for them from the primitive forms. Consequently, only a few of these simple derivatives have been included in *Most-Used Words and Phrases.* However, all derivatives that present some stenographic problems are given.

Selection of Phrases

The shorthand phrases in *Most-Used Words and Phrases* have been selected from a business-letter phrase-frequency count in which the authors analyzed the phrase content of 2,500 business letters containing more than 250,000 words. In this study the authors found 3,536 different phrases, 1,569 of which have been selected for inclusion in the lists of this book. Each phrase, with its shorthand outline, is listed in the lesson where it can first be written.

Distribution of Words and Phrases

As a result of the elimination of a number of word-building and phrasing principles, brief forms, and word beginnings and endings from the system, hundreds of additional useful business words and phrases can now be written in the early lessons of *Gregg Shorthand, Diamond Jubilee Series*. The availability of these additional words and phrases makes possible the construction of smooth, natural practice material almost from the first lesson.

Distribution of Words and Phrases

CHAPTER	WORDS	PHRASES
1	939	347
2	525	536
3	561	268
4	580	162
5	526	105
6	302	129
7	239	9
8	150	13
Totals	3,822	1,569

500 Most Frequently Used Business Words

A feature that teachers will find helpful is the list of the 500 most frequently used business words of the Horn-Peterson study presented in the order of their frequency. This list appears in the Appendix.

Index

At the back of *Most-Used Words and Phrases* is an alphabetical index of all words included in the book, together with an indication of the lesson in which they appear.

It is the hope of the authors that teachers will find the lists in *Most-Used Words and Phrases, Diamond Jubilee Series*, useful in their shorthand teaching.

LOUIS A. LESLIE
CHARLES E. ZOUBEK

Chapter
1

Lesson 1

▶ **S-Z, A, F, V**

| face | safe | say |
| phase | save | vase |

▶ **E**

| easy | fees | see |
| fee | sea | sees |

▶ **N**

| knee | sane | seen |
| navy | scene | vain |

▶ **M**

| aim | may | mean |
| main | me | same |

▶ **T**

ate	meat	stain
east	neat	stay
faced	safety	tea
feet	seat	team

▶ **D**

aid		deed		need	
date		feed		saved	
day		made		stayed	

Lesson 2

▶ **O**

foe		phone		stove	
know		sew		stow	
known		snow		toe	
no		so		vote	
note		stone		zone	

▶ **R**

dear		near		store	
door		nor		storm	
drain		or		story	
drove		rate		tore	
fair		read		torn	
free		remain		trade	
freight		rename		treat	
more		road		wrote	

▶ **L**

deal		late		mail	
fail		lead		real	
feel		leave		relay	
floor		loan		retail	
lady		low		steal	

▶ **H**

hair		hear		hole	
haste		heat		home	
hate		heed		horn	
he		here		whole	

▶ **WORD ENDING** -*ing*

aiming		mailing		reading	
feeling		rating		trading	

▶ **Ī**

die		life		my	
drive		light		night	
dry		line		rely	
dye		lining		right	
file		might		side	
height		mighty		sign	
hide		mile		style	
iron		mine		tire	

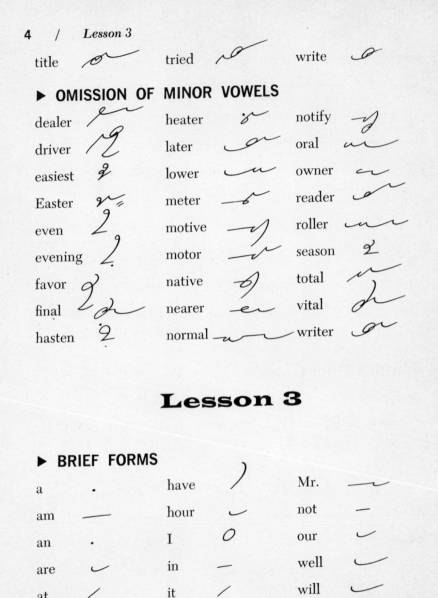

title   tried   write

▶ OMISSION OF MINOR VOWELS

dealer		heater		notify	
driver		later		oral	
easiest		lower		owner	
Easter		meter		reader	
even		motive		roller	
evening		motor		season	
favor		native		total	
final		nearer		vital	
hasten		normal		writer	

Lesson 3

▶ BRIEF FORMS

a		have		Mr.	
am		hour		not	
an		I		our	
are		in		well	
at		it		will	

▶ PHRASES

Have

have made   have not   he may have

he will have    I have tried   may have

I have   I may have   might have

I have made   I will have   will have

I have not   it will have   will not have

I

I am   I mean   I say

I drove   I might   I see

I fear   I need   I will

I feel   I need not   I will not

I know   I remain   I wrote

Will, Well

he will   so well   will not

he will not   well known   will write

Miscellaneous

in it   it will   may not

in our   it will not   might not

▶ LEFT S-Z

dates   frames   knows

days   frozen   ladies

fails   highest   lease

favors   homes   leasing

feels   hours   least

files   its   lines

means		readers		series	
most		realize		sides	
names		release		slight	
needs		rights		source	
niece		rise		styles	
notes		rose		wholesale	
ours		sales		wills	
raise		seats		writers	
rates		seems		zeal	

▶ **P**

deep		plain		proposed	
hope		plate		provide	
open		please		ropes	
paid		pleased		soap	
pair		pleasing		space	
paper		pole		spare	
pay		post		speed	
payroll		premium		supplied	
pays		prepare		suppose	
people		private		supposed	
piece		proceed		supreme	
pipes		promote		type	
place		propose		typewriter	

▶ **B**

able		bolt		buyer	
base		bone		label	
bear		born		labor	
bearing		brief		library	
blame		bright		neighbors	
boats		buy		probate	

▶ **PHRASES**

at least		I realize		in its	
he knows		I suppose		will pay	
he needs		I will see		will see	

Lesson 4

▶ **SH**

shade		share		sheets	
shades		shares		show	
shape		she		shown	
shaped		sheep		shows	

▶ **CH**

chain		cheap		chief	
chains		cheaper		chose	
chair		cheese		chosen	

| each | _(shorthand)_ | reach | _(shorthand)_ | reaches | _(shorthand)_ |
| porch | _(shorthand)_ | reached | _(shorthand)_ | torch | _(shorthand)_ |

▶ J

age	_(shorthand)_	changed	_(shorthand)_	pages	_(shorthand)_
agencies	_(shorthand)_	changes	_(shorthand)_	rage	_(shorthand)_
agency	_(shorthand)_	oblige	_(shorthand)_	range	_(shorthand)_
aging	_(shorthand)_	obliged	_(shorthand)_	siege	_(shorthand)_
change	_(shorthand)_	page	_(shorthand)_	storage	_(shorthand)_

▶ PHRASES

| each day | _(shorthand)_ | each night | _(shorthand)_ | he reaches | _(shorthand)_ |

▶ OO

blue	_(shorthand)_	July	_(shorthand)_	prove	_(shorthand)_
boots	_(shorthand)_	June	_(shorthand)_	proved	_(shorthand)_
choose	_(shorthand)_	juries	_(shorthand)_	proven	_(shorthand)_
do	_(shorthand)_	jury	_(shorthand)_	prune	_(shorthand)_
drew	_(shorthand)_	juvenile	_(shorthand)_	remove	_(shorthand)_
fireproof	_(shorthand)_	loose	_(shorthand)_	roof	_(shorthand)_
food	_(shorthand)_	lose	_(shorthand)_	room	_(shorthand)_
fruit	_(shorthand)_	move	_(shorthand)_	root	_(shorthand)_
hereto	_(shorthand)_	noon	_(shorthand)_	route	_(shorthand)_
jewel	_(shorthand)_	pool	_(shorthand)_	routine	_(shorthand)_
jewelers	_(shorthand)_	poor	_(shorthand)_	rule	_(shorthand)_
jewelry	_(shorthand)_	proof	_(shorthand)_	shoe	_(shorthand)_

shoes		too		two	
spoon		tool		who	
sure		tour		whom	
to		true		whose	

▶ K

acre		corn		make	
bouquet		corner		makes	
break		coupon		making	
broke		course		reclaim	
cake		courtesy		recline	
came		cream		remake	
care		cried		retake	
case		crude		sake	
cave		cry		scheme	
claim		decay		school	
claims		declare		score	
clean		decline		screw	
clear		decrease		smoke	
clearer		keep		specific	
close		keys		spoke	
coal		lake		take	
coast		like		taken	
cool		locate		vacancies	

▶ **G** *(Gay)*

gain	go	gross
gale	goes	group
game	going	grouped
gauge	grade	grow
gave	grades	grown
gay	grading	guide
gear	gray	legal
girls	green	mortgage
gleam	greeting	organ
glued	grew	regain

▶ **PHRASES**

Do

do it	do so	I do not say
do not	I do	I do not see
do not have	I do not	

Sure

feel sure	feeling sure	I am sure

To

to care	to climb	to grow
to claim	to close	to it
to clean	to gain	to its
to clear	to go	to keep

| to take | to tie | to try |
| to taste | to train | to whom |

Who

who are	who knows	who may
who do not	who like	who might
who go	who made	who might have
who have	who make	who takes
who have made	who makes	who will

Miscellaneous

each case	he goes	I like
gave me	he liked	I make
he came	I came	in case
he gave	I gave	it will prove

Lesson 5

▶ Ă

abnormal	active	advance
absence	activity	advice
absorb	acts	advocate
accrued	add	again
accurate	adding	against
act	adhere	aggregate

ago	astray	casting
agree	attached	catch
alone	attractive	chairman
ample	average	chance
amplify	back	class
apiece	backed	classified
appeal	backs	cordial
appear	bad	cracked
applies	bag	data
apply	baggage	draft
approach	bags	drag
approached	balance	fabric
approval	barrel	fact
approve	battery	factory
approved	black	facts
arrange	branch	fast
arrive	branches	flag
arrives	campaign	flat
as	capacity	gas
aside	capital	gasoline
ask	carry	glance
assurance	cash	glass
assure	cashier	graphs
assures	cast	gratified

gratifying		map		ratify	
habit		maps		sacrifice	
had		master		sad	
half		match		salary	
happen		matches		salesman	
happens		material		sample	
happy		matters		sash	
has		narrower		scrap	
hats		package		sedan	
jam		paragraph		staff	
lack		pass		stamp	
lamps		passed		tags	
last		past		task	
lasting		plan		track	
lasts		plans		tract	
machine		proposal		tractor	
machines		rag		traffic	
magazine		ran		traveler	
man		rapid		vast	

▶ Ä

alarm		army		car	
arm		art		cargo	
arms		bargain		carload	

charge	farms	marked
charged	harm	marks
charges	jar	park
charming	large	sharp
dark	March	star
far	margin	start
farm	mark	starts

▶ Ĕ

accept	check	errors
address	checked	establishing
addressed	checks	etc.
any	chest	federal
assets	closest	fell
basket	currency	fellow
bed	desk	fellows
beg	edges	finest
belt	effect	fresh
best	effective	get
better	elect	getting
bread	else	guess
cabinet	enable	harvest
cancel	enamel	head
cheapest	error	heads

heartless	medal	select
heavy	medicine	seller
help	messages	sells
helped	met	semester
helpless	metal	sense
helplessness	nearest	separate
helps	needless	set
hopeless	negative	settle
hotel	net	shell
jelly	parcel	shelves
kept	pleasure	sketch
largest	pledge	slightest
latest	presence	slowest
led	pressure	specified
left	professor	specify
leg	protect	spread
less	protest	step
lessons	ready	supremacy
let	regret	telegraph
letter	relative	telephone
letters	remedy	tell
lowest	rest	test
market	said	testify
measure	secretary	tests

treasure		treasury		verify	
treasurer		verified		wrenches	

▶ ĭ

admit		dictate		hit	
April		did		if	
arisen		dig		ignore	
artist		dishes		illness	
been		drastic		imagine	
benefit		drill		inactive	
bid		elastic		kill	
bidding		facilitate		kitchen	
bids		familiar		liberal	
billing		fill		liberty	
bills		finance		list	
bridge		finish		listen	
bridges		fiscal		little	
built		fit		live	
busy		gift		lives	
chemistry		give		merit	
chickens		given		middle	
Christmas		gives		milk	
cigars		guilty		mill	
city		him		miss	
clipping		hinges		notice	

omit	principal	since
original	prohibit	sincere
pencil	remit	solicit
pick	rid	spirit
pig	risk	statistics
pigs	river	still
pin	ship	territory
pins	shipped	tickets
practice	shipper	tip
predict	sickness	trip
prettiest	similar	vicinity
pretty	simple	visit

▶ **OBSCURE VOWEL**

answer	first	major
certificate	fur	prefer
certified	grocery	search
certify	her	serve
church	hosiery	service
circle	hurry	surprise
clerk	hurt	surprised
earn	journal	teacher
earnest	larger	teachers
firm	learn	tracer
firms	ledger	urge

▶ **OVER** *Th*

bath		smooth		thick	
blacksmith		teeth		thicker	
booth		theater		thickness	
death		theme		thin	
faith		then		thinner	
method		these		tooth	

▶ **UNDER** *Th*

birth		health		thread	
birthday		healthy		three	
both		lathe		throat	
clothing		north		through	
earth		thorough		throw	
growth		though		thrown	

▶ **PHRASES**

as if		asking me		has had	
as it		at last		has known	
as it will		at these		has made	
as these		did not		has met	
as though		give me		has no	
as to		had not		has not	
as well		has given		have given	

have had	I have had	since then
he did	I left	so large
he did not	I live	these are
he fell	I met	through its
he felt	I notice	through these
he gets	I ran	to cancel
he left	I read	to carry
he lives	I said	to cash
he said	if it	to catch
I did	if my	to get
I did not	if so	to give
I felt	if these	to tell
I get	in fact	to these
I give	in these	to travel
I guess	it has	who have had

▶ BRIEF FORMS

but	is	with
can	Mrs.	withdrew
cannot	of	you
can't	that	your
his	the	yours

▶ PHRASES

Can

can have	he can	he can make

he can't	I cannot	who can
I can	I can see	who cannot

Is, His

as it is	if it is	it is
he is	in his	she is
he is not	is it	she is not
he is the	is not	to his
here is	is the	who is

Of

of his	of its	of the
of it	of our	of these

That

as that	is that	that have
as to that	is that the	that is
ask that	of that	that is not
at that	realize that	that is the
hope that	so that	that it
hope that the	so that the	that it has
hoping that	that are	that it is
if that is	that are not	that it will
in that	that do not	that its

that may	that these	through that
that our	that will	to that
that the	that will not	with that

The

as the	has the	make the
as to the	if the	realize the
ask the	in the	through the
at the	in the last	to the

With

with him	with our	with the

You

as you	ask you	if you can
as you are	asking you	if you cannot
as you can	can you	if you care
as you did	do you	if you did not
as you go	give you	if you do
as you have	giving you	if you do not
as you know	have you	if you get
as you may	hope you will	if you go
as you may have	if you	if you have
as you say	if you are	if you have not
as you will	if you are not	if you know
as you will see	if you are sure	if you let

if you need	you cannot	you may
if you see	you cannot see	you may have
if you will	you can't	you may not
if you will have	you did	you might
if you will see	you did not	you might have
of you	you do	you might not
reach you	you do not	you need
serving you	you have	you need not
to you	you have had	you say
with you	you have made	you see
you are	you have not	you will
you are not	you have seen	you will have
you can	you know	you will not
you can have	you made	you will not have
you can see	you make	you will see

Your

as to your	if your	with your
as your	of your	your letter
ask your	of yours	your name
have your	to your	your needs

Chapter

2

Lesson 7

▶ ŏ

adopt·	copper	golf
anybody	correct	got
block	cost	hog
blotter	costing	holiday
body	costs	honest
borrow	cottage	honesty
borrowers	crop	honor
bronze	cross	hop
catalogue	crossed	hospital
clock	dock	hot
collar	doctor	job
collect	dog	jobber
college	dollar	knowledge
co-operate	drop	lobby
co-operative	follow	lock
copies	foreign	logs

23

loss	often	promised
lost	oftener	proper
lot	on	property
mob	operate	prospect
model	opposed	prospective
moderate	opposite	remodeling
modify	orange	rob
mop	origin	rock
moral	pocket	rod
nobody	policy	shop
observe	polish	soft
occur	politics	solid
occurrence	popular	solve
off	positive	sorrow
offer	problem	spot
office	profit	stock
officers	project	stop
offset	promise	top

▶ **AW**

abroad	ball	broader
all	baseball	brought
author	bought	call
authoritative	broad	caught
auto	broadcasting	cause

caused	fault	saw
clause	jaw	small
daughter	laws	smaller
draw	ought	talked
drawer	raw	taught
drawn	recall	thought
fall	salt	vault

▶ PHRASES

across the	I talked	on that day
has taught	I thought	on the
he calls	off the	on these
he got	on his	on your
he lost	on it	to call
he saw	on its	to cause
he talked	on our	to collect
I call	on sale	to correct
I got	on that	to talk
I saw	on that date	who taught

▶ SPECIAL BUSINESS FORMS

Dear Madam	My dear Sir	Yours truly
Dear Sir	Sincerely yours	Yours very truly

Lesson 8

▶ BRIEF FORMS

be		goods		therefore	
before		put		therein	
being		shall		thereon	
by		their		this	
for		there		which	
good		thereby		would	

▶ PHRASES

Be

be sure		if it will be		that will be	
being sure		if you can be		who can be	
can be		if you will be		who may be	
can be sure		it will be		who might be	
cannot be		it will not be		who will be	
can't be		may be		will be	
he can be		may not be		will not be	
he will be		might be		would be	
he would be		might not be		would not be	
I can be		need be		you can be	
I cannot be		need not be		you may be	
I can't be		she may be		you may be sure	
I will be		that it will be		you will be	
I would be		that may be		you will not be	

By

by it		by that		by which	
by its		by the		by you	
by mail		by these		by your	

For

for his		for that		for whom	
for it		for the		for you	
for its		for the last		for your	
for me		for the past		for your letter	
for Mr.		for their		before that	
for most		for these		before the	
for my		for which		before you	
for our		for which the		before your	

Good

as good		good deal	

Shall

I shall		I shall make		shall not	
I shall be		I shall not		shall not be	
I shall have		I shall see		you shall have	

There, their

as there		if there is		of their	
as there is		if there will		that their	
if there are		is there		that there are	

that there is	there may	there will be
there are	there may be	there would be
there is	there will	to their

This

as this	in this case	this is the
at this	in this matter	this letter
before this	of this	this man
by this	on this	this matter
do this	on this matter	this may
for this	since this	this may be
hope that this	that this	this means
if this	that this is	this will
if this is	this can be	this would
if this is not	this date	this would be
if this is the	this is	to this
in this	this is not	with this

Which

in which	on which the	which means
in which the	which is	which you
in which you	which is the	which you can
of which	which may	which you may
on which	which may be	with which

Would

| as you would | he would | I would |
| as you would be | he would have | I would have |

I would not	that would be	would have
if you would	who would	you would
if you would be	who would be	you would be
if you would have	who would have	you would have
that would	who would not	you would not

▶ WORD ENDING -*ly*

actively	finally	nicely
amply	firmly	normally
badly	freely	only
barely	highly	originally
briefly	honestly	positively
clearly	inevitably	possibly
closely	largely	principally
cordially	lately	properly
correctly	legally	rapidly
costly	likely	rarely
daily	locally	separately
deeply	mainly	simply
earlier	manly	sincerely
earliest	materially	slightly
early	merely	strictly
earnestly	mostly	surely
fairly	namely	thoroughly
favorably	nearly	totally

Lesson 9

▶ **WORD ENDING** *-tion*

action	mission	profession
allocation	motion	professional
application	national	promotion
authorization	nationally	proportion
cancellation	obligation	proportionate
caution	occasion	proposition
collection	occasionally	propositions
collision	operation	protection
co-operation	option	provision
corporation	physician	ration
correction	portion	relation
declaration	position	section
election	possession	sectional
eradication	precaution	selection
fashion	preparation	session
irrigation	prescription	supposition
location	prevention	vacation

▶ **WORD ENDINGS** *-cient, -ciency*

ancient	efficient	proficiency
efficiency	patient	proficient

▶ **WORD ENDING** *-tial*

beneficial	especially	essential

essentially	initial	partial
financial	initialed	social
financially	official	special

▶ *To* **FOLLOWED BY A DOWNSTROKE**

as to be	to farm	to prepare
has to be	to feel	to preserve
is to be	to fill	to proceed
to balance	to finance	to promote
to be	to finish	to protect
to be sure	to fit	to protest
to bear	to fly	to prove
to beat	to follow	to provide
to bite	to have	to put
to blame	to have you	to say
to borrow	to jar	to see
to break	to park	to select
to burn	to pass	to sell
to buy	to pay	to separate
to change	to pick	to serve
to charge	to place	to serve you
to check	to plan	to share
to choose	to play	to ship
to face	to please	to shoot
to fall	to post	to show

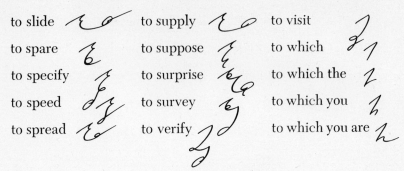

to slide	to supply	to visit
to spare	to suppose	to which
to specify	to surprise	to which the
to speed	to survey	to which you
to spread	to verify	to which you are

Lesson 10

▶ **ND**

assigned	end	lend
band	fastened	lined
bind	find	loaned
binder	friend	mind
bindery	gained	opened
bond	grand	owned
bonded	grind	pending
brand	happened	phoned
burned	island	planned
calendar	kind	remainder
candy	kindest	remained
canned	kindness	remind
cleaned	land	reminded
cylinder	lands	render
earned	learned	sand

signed	splendid	trained
spend	surrender	trend

▶ NT

absent	current	plenty
agent	event	prevent
agents	genteel	prevented
apparent	gentle	printer
applicant	grant	rent
aunt	granted	rental
bent	guarantee	rented
carpenter	hints	sent
cent	paint	silent
center	parents	spent
central	plant	talent
centralized	planted	urgent
cogent	pleasant	vacant

Ant-, End-, Ent-

anticipate	entire	indications
anticipation	entirely	intact
antique	entry	intelligence
endorse	indicate	intelligent
endorsed	indicates	intelligently
endorser	indication	into

▶ **PHRASES**

aren't	I learned	to plant
as you will find	I sent	to prevent
didn't	if you didn't	to print
don't	if you don't	to spend
hadn't	into it	who didn't
hasn't	into that	who isn't
haven't	into the	will find
he didn't	into these	wouldn't
he finds	into this	you aren't
he isn't	isn't	you didn't
I didn't	isn't it	you don't
I don't	to bind	you haven't
I find	to find	you will find
I haven't	to paint	you wouldn't

▶ **SES**

access	auspices	chances
addresses	balances	classes
advances	bases	clauses
advices	basis	closes
analysis	braces	courses
arises	cases	criticism
assessed	causes	faces
assist	census	finances

glasses		nurses		proposes	
horses		offices		releases	
leases		passes		says	
lenses		places		services	
losses		premises		sister	
mattresses		presses		sizes	
necessary		prices		sources	
necessitate		process		spaces	
necessity		processes		suspend	
notices		promises		versus	

Lesson 11

▶ BRIEF FORMS

and		hands		them	
could		handle		they	
from		send		was	
hand		should		when	

▶ PHRASES

And

and are		and our		and the	
and have		and say		and their	
and his		and see		and they	
and is		and that		and was	
and let		and that is		and which	

and will *[shorthand]*   and will be *[shorthand]*   and will not *[shorthand]*

Could

could be *[shorthand]*	I could *[shorthand]*	who could *[shorthand]*
could not *[shorthand]*	I could be *[shorthand]*	you could *[shorthand]*
could not be *[shorthand]*	I could not *[shorthand]*	you could be *[shorthand]*
he could *[shorthand]*	I could see *[shorthand]*	you could have *[shorthand]*
he could not *[shorthand]*	I couldn't *[shorthand]*	you could not *[shorthand]*
he couldn't *[shorthand]*	if you could *[shorthand]*	you could see *[shorthand]*

From

from him *[shorthand]*	from that *[shorthand]*	from this *[shorthand]*
from his *[shorthand]*	from the *[shorthand]*	from you *[shorthand]*
from it *[shorthand]*	from them *[shorthand]*	from which *[shorthand]*
from our *[shorthand]*	from these *[shorthand]*	hear from you *[shorthand]*

Send

send him *[shorthand]*	send this *[shorthand]*	sending the *[shorthand]*
send them *[shorthand]*	send you *[shorthand]*	sending you *[shorthand]*

Should

he should *[shorthand]*	I should like *[shorthand]*	who should *[shorthand]*
he should be *[shorthand]*	I should say *[shorthand]*	who should be *[shorthand]*
he should have *[shorthand]*	should be *[shorthand]*	you should *[shorthand]*
I should *[shorthand]*	should have *[shorthand]*	you should be *[shorthand]*
I should be *[shorthand]*	should not be *[shorthand]*	you should have *[shorthand]*
I should have *[shorthand]*	shouldn't *[shorthand]*	you should not *[shorthand]*

Them

ask them	into them	through them
for them	of them	to them
in them	on them	with them

They

as they	they are	they don't
as they are	they are not	they have
before they	they can	they may
if they	they can be	they may be
if they are	they can have	they will
if they are not	they cannot	they will be
if they can	they can't	they will have
if they would	they could	they will not
if they would be	they could not	they will see
that they	they did	they would
that they are	they do	they would not
that they will	they do not	they would not be

Was

he was	it wasn't	this was the
he wasn't	that it was	was it
I was	that there was	was that
it was	there was	was the
it was the	this was	which was

When

when our   *[shorthand]*   when the   *[shorthand]*   when they   *[shorthand]*

when that   *[shorthand]*   when these   *[shorthand]*   when this   *[shorthand]*

▶ RD

accordance	*[sh]*	guard	*[sh]*	pardoned	*[sh]*
answered	*[sh]*	hard	*[sh]*	preferred	*[sh]*
appeared	*[sh]*	harder	*[sh]*	prepared	*[sh]*
assured	*[sh]*	hardly	*[sh]*	record	*[sh]*
bird	*[sh]*	hazard	*[sh]*	rendered	*[sh]*
board	*[sh]*	heard	*[sh]*	retired	*[sh]*
border	*[sh]*	hired	*[sh]*	seaboard	*[sh]*
burden	*[sh]*	ignored	*[sh]*	stored	*[sh]*
card	*[sh]*	occurred	*[sh]*	surrendered	*[sh]*
cord	*[sh]*	offered	*[sh]*	third	*[sh]*
favored	*[sh]*	orchard	*[sh]*	tired	*[sh]*
garden	*[sh]*	pardon	*[sh]*	toward	*[sh]*

▶ LD

billed	*[sh]*	children	*[sh]*	filed	*[sh]*
build	*[sh]*	cold	*[sh]*	filled	*[sh]*
builders	*[sh]*	drilled	*[sh]*	fold	*[sh]*
called	*[sh]*	entitled	*[sh]*	folded	*[sh]*
canceled	*[sh]*	failed	*[sh]*	folder	*[sh]*
child	*[sh]*	field	*[sh]*	gold	*[sh]*

golden	holds	rolled
handled	mailed	sealed
hauled	milled	settled
held	old	shoulder
hold	older	sold
holders	oldest	told

▶ PHRASES

Rd

| to board | to burden | to pardon |

Ld

has called	he told	I traveled
he called	I called	old-fashioned
he sold	I told	to build

▶ *Been* IN PHRASES

could have been	have not been	there have been
had been	having been	to have been
had not been	I have been	which have been
has been	it has been	would have been
has not been	should have been	you have been
have been	there has been	you have not been

▶ *Able* IN PHRASES

| be able | being able | has not been able |
| been able | has been able | have not been able |

he may be able

he should be able

he will be able

he will not be able

he would be able

I have not been able

I shall be able

I shall not be able

I will be able

to be able

will be able

you may be able

you should be able

you will be able

you would be able

Chapter
3

Lesson 13

▶ **BRIEF FORMS**

enclose	⌐	orders	↗	were	e
enclosed	↗	soon	↙	work	⌒
enclosure	⌐ɳ	sooner	↙	worked	⌒
glad	⌒	thank	⌐	worker	⌒
gladly	⌒ₒ	thanked	⌐	year	e
order	↗	thanks	⌐	years	eₗ
ordered	↗	very	⌡	yesterday	⌡

▶ **PHRASES**

Enclose

he enclosed ;↗ I enclose ⌐ you enclosed ↗

Glad

be glad ⌒ I am glad ⌒ shall be glad ⌡

he will be glad ℓ⌒ I shall be glad ⌡ they will be glad ℓ

he would be glad ·⌒ I should be glad ⌡ will be glad ⌒

Order

in order ↗ in order that ↗ in order that the ↗

41

Thank

thank you	thank you for the	thank you for your
thank you for	thank you for this	to thank you for

Very

| very glad | very good | very well |

Were

| if it were | there were | were not |

▶ U

above	colored	famous
adjust	couple	hunting
adjusts	cover	illustrate
ambitious	covered	illustration
annum	covers	illustrations
apparatus	cup	industry
blood	cups	just
bonus	cut	justice
bud	does	justified
bulbs	drug	justify
bulk	duck	justly
bus	dug	luck
butter	dust	mud
chorus	enormous	muslin
color	enough	nervous

none	reduction	sufficient
number	religious	thus
numbered	rough	tough
nut	rub	truck
oven	rubber	trust
plug	shovels	unable
plus	status	uneven
product	stuff	up
production	suction	upper
productive	suffer	us
prosperous	suffered	utterly

▶ ōō

book	foot	pull
booked	full	pulled
bookkeeping	fully	push
booklet	hook	stood
bushel	look	sugar
cook	looked	took

▶ PHRASES

Does

does not	he does	this does not
does not have	he does not	who doesn't
doesn't	that does not	which does

Us

before us		gave us		send us	
by us		give us		sending us	
for us		giving us		to give us	
from us		on us		with us	

Miscellaneous

above the		I took		to cut	
he looks		I trust		to fuss	
he took		to book		to push	
I look		to cover		to trust	

▶ W

Wa

highway		waiver		wear	
wages		waste		wears	
wagon		wave		weigh	
waist		way		weighed	
wait		ways		weight	

We

we		wet		witness	
weak		width		word	
week		win		worries	
went		wind		worse	
west		winter		worst	

Wi

| wide | wire | wise |
| wife | wired | wives |

Wo

walk	war	water
wall	warm	woe
walnut	warrant	won't
want	wash	worn
wanted	watch	woven

Woo

| wonder | wood | wool |
| wondering | woods | woolen |

▶ SW

swam	sweet	swivel
swear	swell	swollen
sweater	switch	sworn

▶ PHRASES

We

as we	if we can be	if we have
as we are	if we cannot	we are
as we have	if we could	we are not
if we	if we do	we are sure
if we can	if we don't	we call

we can	we feel sure	we mean
we can be	we filled	we might
we can have	we find	we might be able
we can make	we get	we need
we can say	we give	we note
we cannot	we got	we notice
we cannot be	we have	we shall
we can't	we have been	we shall be
we could	we have been able	we shall be able
we could be	we have given	we shall be glad
we could have	we have had	we shall have
we could not	we have made	we shall mail
we couldn't	we have not	we shall make
we did	we have not been	we shall need
we did not	we have not been able	we shall not
we didn't	we have not had	we shall not be able
we do	we know	we shall see
we do not	we made	we should
we do not say	we mailed	we should be
we do not see	we make	we should have
we don't	we may	we should like
we enclose	we may be	we should not like
we failed	we may be able	we should say
we feel	we may have	we shouldn't

we take	we will	we would be glad
we thank you for	we will be	we would have
we thank you for the	we will have	we would like
we thank you for your	we will not	we would not
we took	we will not be	we would not be able
we tried	we will see	we wouldn't
we trust	we would	which we
we try	we would be	which we are

Lesson 14

▶ WH

whale		wheel		whip	
wheat		while		white	

▶ THE SOUND OF *W* IN THE BODY OF A WORD

acquainted	likewise	quota
adequate	liquid	quote
always	queen	railway
Broadway	query	requisition
dwelling	quick	roadway
equip	quicker	square
equipped	quickest	squarely
hardware	quit	twice
inadequate	quite	twin

▶ TED

accepted		hesitated		protested	
acted		homestead		quoted	
adapted		illustrated		rated	
adjusted		indicated		related	
admitted		lifted		remitted	
adopted		limited		rested	
affected		liquidated		routed	
anticipated		listed		selected	
asserted		located		separated	
attested		marketed		solicited	
benefited		neglected		started	
coasted		noted		steady	
collected		omitted		tested	
co-operated		operated		treated	
corrected		pasted		visited	
dated		posted		waited	
fitted		protected		wasted	

Others

studied		study		today	

▶ DED

added		deduct		deduction	
dead		deducted		deductions	

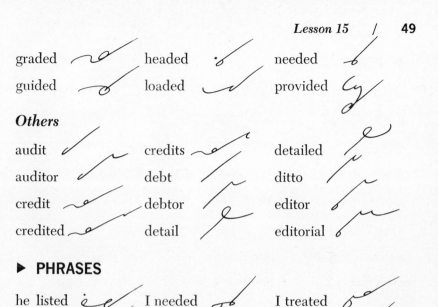

graded	headed	needed
guided	loaded	provided

Others

audit	credits	detailed
auditor	debt	ditto
credit	debtor	editor
credited	detail	editorial

▶ **PHRASES**

he listed	I needed	I treated
he needed	I noted	we quoted

Lesson 15

▶ **BRIEF FORMS**

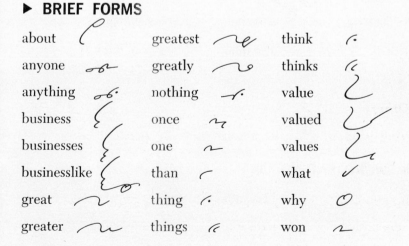

about	greatest	think
anyone	greatly	thinks
anything	nothing	value
business	once	valued
businesses	one	values
businesslike	than	what
great	thing	why
greater	things	won

▶ **PHRASES**

About

about it		about the		about which	
about its		about them		about you	
about my		about these		about your	
about that		about this			

One

any one		one thing		one year	
each one		one-half		only one	
for one		one way		this one	

Than

less than		less than the		than the

Thing, Think

as you think		if they think		to think	
do you think		if you think		we do not think	
I do not think		same thing		who think	
I think		they think		you think	

What

what are		what is		what will	
what has been		what is the		what will be	

▶ **WORD ENDING** -ble

acceptable		adjustable		agreeable	
adaptable		advisable		applicable	

appreciable	eligible	possible
available	equitable	profitable
cable	favorable	reliable
capable	feasible	salable
double	liable	table
doubled	payable	trouble

▶ WORD BEGINNING *Re-*

reappear	refers	resale
reason	refining	research
reasonable	reflect	reservation
reasonably	reflected	reserve
reasons	region	reserved
rebate	register	reservoir
receipt	registered	resist
receive	rejected	resources
recent	repair	respect
reception	repaired	respectively
rechecked	repeat	respondent
reciprocate	repeated	response
refer	repeatedly	reveal
reference	replace	reverse
referred	replied	revise
referring	reproduction	revision

Lesson 16

▶ **OI**

annoyance		coin		oil	
annoyed		corduroy		point	
appointed		hoist		poison	
avoid		join		royal	
boiled		joined		soil	
boiler		joint		soiled	
boy		jointly		spoiled	
boys		joy		toy	
choice		loyal		voice	
coil		noise		void	

▶ **PHRASES**

to boil	to join	to point

▶ **MAN**

manage	managers	romance
manager	manner	woman

▶ **MEN**

amend	immensely	mental
amended	many	mentally
cement	meant	mention
freshmen	men	mentioned

salesmen ___   tremendous ___   women ___

▶ MIN

administer ___   mineral ___   prominence ___

aluminum ___   minute ___   prominent ___

eliminate ___   nominal ___   prominently ___

▶ MON

harmonize ___   lemon ___   month ___

harmony ___   money ___   monthly ___

▶ MEM, MUM

member ___   memorial ___   minimum ___

memo ___   memory ___   remember ___

▶ PHRASES

as many ___   I mention ___   these men ___

each month ___   I mentioned ___   this month ___

few minutes ___   in this manner ___   to mention ___

few months ___   in this month's ___   we mention ___

he mentioned ___   so many ___   you mentioned ___

▶ WORD BEGINNING *Be-*

became ___   begins ___   believer ___

because ___   behalf ___   below ___

began ___   behind ___   besides ___

begin ___   belief ___   betray ___

beginning ___   believe ___   beyond ___

Lesson 17

▶ BRIEF FORMS

elsewhere	manufacture	those
gentleman	manufactured	where
gentlemen	manufacturer	whereabouts
importance	morning	whereas
important	nowhere	wherein

▶ PHRASES

Those

about those	for those	to those
and those	from those	when those
as those	in those	with those
at those	of those	
by those	that those	

Miscellaneous

this morning   very important   we manufacture

▶ WORD BEGINNING *Per-*

per	permanent	personnel
percentage	permit	persons
perfect	permitted	persuade
perfectly	person	persuaded
perforated	personal	persuades
perhaps	personally	persuasion

▶ **WORD BEGINNING** *Pur-*

purchase   purchases   purloin
purchased   purchasing   purple

▶ **PHRASES**

per cent   per month   to persuade
per hour   to permit   to purchase

▶ **WORD BEGINNING** *De-*

debit	deliveries	depot
decide	depend	derive
decided	dependable	deserve
decidedly	depended	design
decision	dependent	designed
delay	depends	designer
delayed	depleted	designs
delays	deposit	desirable
deliberate	deposited	desire
delighted	depositor	desired
deliver	depository	desires
delivered	deposits	desirous

▶ **WORD BEGINNING** *Dĭ-*

diligently   directed   directly
direct   direction   director

▶ PHRASES

he decided	if you decide	we desire
he desires	if you desire	we have decided
I decided	we decide	who desire
I desire	we decided	you desire

Chapter

4

Lesson 19

▶ **BRIEF FORMS**

accompanied	hereafter	present
advertise	immediate	presented
after	immediately	represent
aftermath	must	representative
afternoon	opportunity	represented
afterthought	part	represents
companies	participate	wish
company	parties	wished
departing	party	wishes

▶ **PHRASES**

After

after that	after them	after this
after the	after these	after which

Must

he must	he must be	he must have

I must	she must	who must
I must be	she must be	who must be
I must have	that must be	you must
I must say	they must	you must be
must be	we must	you must be able
must have	we must have	you must have

Miscellaneous

at present	if you wish	to part
I wish	on our part	to present

▶ Ū

accusation	human	tube
accuse	peculiar	unique
acute	prosecute	unit
argue	prosecution	unite
beautify	pure	united
bureau	refusal	unusually
cubic	refused	usual
cure	refuses	utilization
few	review	view
fewer	reviews	viewed
fuel	tribune	views

▶ PHRASES

few days	in view	to prosecute
I refuse	to beautify	

► WORD ENDING *-ment*

adjustment	document	movement
advertisement	elementary	nonpayment
agreement	elements	ornamental
allotment	endorsement	payment
amendment	equipment	replacement
appointment	establishment	settlement
arrangement	garment	shipment
assessment	management	supplement
assignment	measurement	supplementary
basement	moment	supplemented
casement	momentary	treatment

► PHRASES

few moments   in payment   to supplement

Lesson 20

► OW

account	aloud	announcement
accountant	amount	announces
accounted	amounted	around
allow	amounts	background
allowance	announce	blouse
allowed	announced	bound

brown	flowers	pound
clown	found	pounds
council	founded	powder
counsel	foundry	power
count	ground	proud
counted	house	round
counter	household	sound
county	houses	south
cow	loud	southeast
crowd	mount	surround
doubt	mounted	towels
doubted	mouth	tower
doubtless	now	town
down	ounce	voucher
flour	plow	warehouse

▶ **PHRASES**

he found	I found	we count
I doubt	in our power	we doubt
I doubted	to count	we found

▶ **WORD ENDING** *-ther*

another	brother	farther
bother	brotherly	father
bothered	either	feather

gather	neither	rather
gathered	other	together
leather	others	weather
mother	otherwise	whether

▶ PHRASES

any other	I gathered	to bother
each other	many other	to gather
he gathered	other than	

▶ WORD BEGINNING *Con-*

concealed	conducted	confusion
concentrate	conductor	congested
conception	confer	congestion
concern	conference	connected
concerned	confess	connection
concerns	confine	connections
concert	confined	conscientious
concession	confirm	consent
conclude	confiscate	conservative
concluded	confiscation	consider
conclusion	conflict	considerably
conclusive	confuse	consideration
concrete	confused	considered
conduct	confusing	consign

consigned	constructive	controversy
consignee	contact	convention
consignment	contest	conversation
consist	contract	conversion
consisted	contracted	convert
consists	contractor	converted
consolidate	contracts	convey
construct	contrary	convince
constructed	contrast	reconcile
construction	control	reconstruction

▶ **WORD BEGINNING** *Com-*

accommodate	committee	competitive
accomplish	commodities	competitor
accomplished	commodity	competitors
combine	common	compiled
comedies	commonly	complaint
command	compact	complete
commence	comparative	completed
commend	compare	completely
comment	compared	completion
commerce	compel	compliment
commercial	compelled	complimentary
commitments	compensation	comply
committed	compete	composed

composer 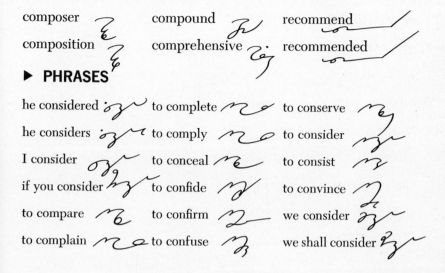 compound   recommend

composition   comprehensive   recommended

▶ PHRASES

he considered	to complete	to conserve
he considers	to comply	to consider
I consider	to conceal	to consist
if you consider	to confide	to convince
to compare	to confirm	we consider
to complain	to confuse	we shall consider

Lesson 21

▶ BRIEF FORMS

advantage	everybody	suggest
advantages	everyone	suggested
big	everything	suggestion
bigger	everywhere	use
bigness	how	used
correspond	out	uselessly
corresponded	outline	uses
correspondence	outlined	whatever
corresponds	outside	whenever
ever	several	wherever
every	such	without

▶ **PHRASES**

Ever, Every

ever since	every minute	everyone
every day	every month	every other

Several

several days	several months	several others
several minutes	several other	

Such

from such	no such	on such
in such	of such	with such

▶ **DEN**

accident	deny	precedent
condense	evidence	president
condensed	evident	residence
confidence	evidently	resident
confident	identified	sudden
confidential	identify	wooden

Others

abandon	danger	dinner
audience	dangerous	guidance

▶ **TEN**

attend	attended	competent
attendance	attention	consistent

consistently	rotten	tend
content	sentence	tendency
contention	stenographer	tender
gotten	stenographic	tendered
maintenance	straighten	tent
patent	straightened	tentative
retention	tenant	written

▶ TAN

acceptance	hesitancy	stand
assistance	outstanding	standard
assistant	remittance	standing
constant	remittances	standpoint
constantly	resistance	stands

▶ TON

button	carton	tonight

▶ TIN

bulletin	contingency	itinerary
continent	contingent	satin

▶ TAIN

ascertain	certainty	curtain
attainment	contain	detained
certain	contained	fountain
certainly	container	maintain

maintained   obtainable   retain

mountain   obtained   sustained

obtain   pertaining   unobtainable

▶ PHRASES

about ten days   fountain pen   ten days

Lesson 22

▶ DEM, ETC.

damage   demonstration   medium

damaged   dimensions   random

demand   domestic   redemption

demonstrate   freedom   seldom

▶ TEM

attempt   contemplated   system

attempted   esteemed   temper

attempting   item   temple

contemplate   itemized   temporary

▶ TIM

estimate   estimates   legitimately

estimated   legitimate   timber

▶ TOM

accustomed   automatic   automobile

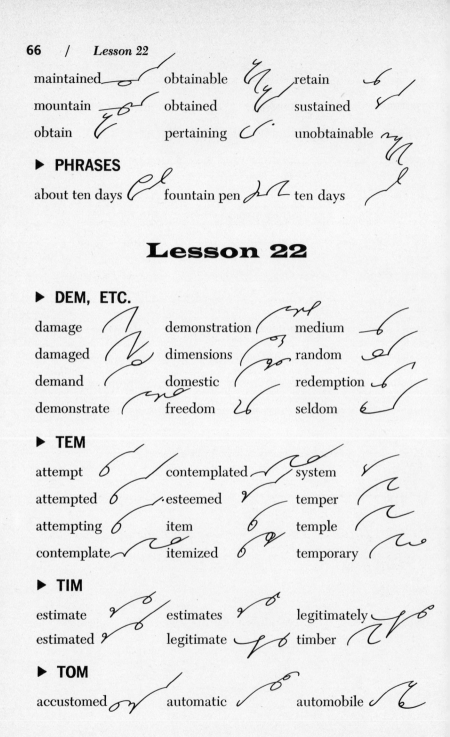

bottom	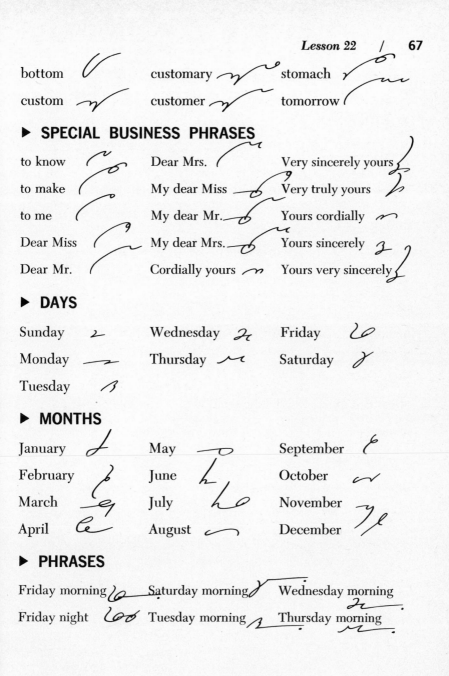	customary		stomach	
custom		customer		tomorrow	

▶ SPECIAL BUSINESS PHRASES

to know		Dear Mrs.		Very sincerely yours	
to make		My dear Miss		Very truly yours	
to me		My dear Mr.		Yours cordially	
Dear Miss		My dear Mrs.		Yours sincerely	
Dear Mr.		Cordially yours		Yours very sincerely	

▶ DAYS

Sunday		Wednesday		Friday	
Monday		Thursday		Saturday	
Tuesday					

▶ MONTHS

January		May		September	
February		June		October	
March		July		November	
April		August		December	

▶ PHRASES

Friday morning		Saturday morning		Wednesday morning	
Friday night		Tuesday morning		Thursday morning	

Lesson 23

▶ BRIEF FORMS

acknowledge	ϱ	over	ν	questions	ϡ
acknowledged	ϱ✓	overburdened	ν	time	(
acknowledgment	ϛ	overcharge	ϟ	timer	(
during	/	overlooked	ν✓	times	(
general	↲	oversight	ϟ	worth	⟋
generally	↲	oversize	ϟ	worthless	⟋
gone	⌐	question	ϡ	worthy	⟋
meantime	⌐	questionable	ϟ	yet	ϛ

▶ PHRASES

Time

about that time	⟋	by the time	⟋	of time	⟋
about the time	⟋	by this time	⟋	on time	⟋
about this time	⟋	each time	⟋	one time	⟋
any time	⟋	few times	⟋	several times	⟋
at that time	⟋	for the time	⟋	since that time	⟋
at the time	⟋	from time	⟋	such time	⟋
at this time	⟋	in time	⟋	that time	⟋
at which time	⟋	many times	⟋	this time	⟋
by that time	⟋	of that time	⟋	to time	⟋

Yet

as yet	ϟ	has not yet been	ϟ	I have not yet	ϟ
has not yet	ϟ	have not yet	ϟ	is not yet	ϟ

Miscellaneous

has gone · ⟋⟍ have gone ⟋⟍ in question ⟍

▶ DEF, DIF

defect ⟋⟍	deferred ⟋2	differ ⟋2
defense ⟋2	definite ⟋2	difference ⟋2
defer ⟋2	defy ⟋2	different ⟋2

▶ DIV, DEV

develop ⟋2	devised ⟋2	diverted ⟋2
developed ⟋2	devote ⟋2	divide ⟋2
development ⟋2	devoted ⟋2	divided ⟋2
develops ⟋2	diversified ⟋2	dividend ⟋2
device ⟋2	diversion ⟋2	division ⟋2
devise ⟋2	divert ⟋2	divisions ⟋2

▶ OMISSION OF *E* FROM *Ū*

absolute	continued	duty
avenue	continues	education
casually	continuous	educational
communicate	due	enumerated
communication	dues	induce
communities	duly	inducement
community	duplicate	issue
continuance	duplicated	issued
continue	duplication	issues

knew	produce	renew
lieu	produced	renewal
manuscript	producers	renewed
monument	produces	revenue
music	pursuant	student
new	pursue	suit
newer	pursued	suitable
newest	pursuit	suited
news	reduce	visual
numerous	reduced	volume
overdue	reduces	volumes

▶ **PHRASES**

he knew	to continue	we continue
I knew	to produce	we knew
in lieu	to pursue	you knew

Chapter
5

Lesson 25

▶ BRIEF FORMS

difficult	requested	statement
difficulty	requests	states
envelope	satisfaction	success
envelopes	satisfactorily	under
estate	satisfactory	undercharges
next	satisfied	undersized
progress	satisfy	understand
progressive	state	understandable
request	stated	understood

▶ PHRASES

Next

next meeting · next morning · next time

next month · next ten days · next year

▶ WORDS MODIFIED IN PHRASES

As soon as

as soon as   as soon as possible   as soon as the

Hope

I hope	I hope to be	we hope the
I hope that	I hope to see	we hope these
I hope that the	we hope	we hope this
I hope the	we hope that	we hope to have
I hope these	we hope that these	we hope you can
I hope this	we hope that this	we hope you will

Us

let us	let us know	let us say
let us have	let us make	to us

To

to do	to do so	to do the
to do it	to do that	to do this

Order

if your order	thank you for your order	your order
of your order	you ordered	your orders

Miscellaneous

of course   of course it is   of course it will

Lesson 26

▶ **ANY VOWEL AFTER THE DIPHTHONG ī**

amplifier   appliance   bias

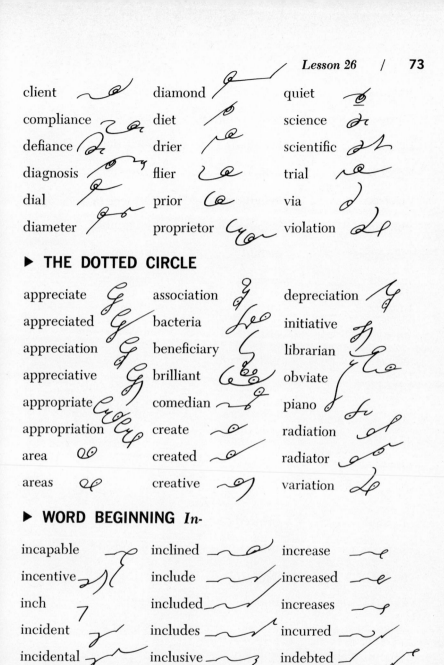

client   diamond   quiet
compliance   diet   science
defiance   drier   scientific
diagnosis   flier   trial
dial   prior   via
diameter   proprietor   violation

▶ THE DOTTED CIRCLE

appreciate   association   depreciation
appreciated   bacteria   initiative
appreciation   beneficiary   librarian
appreciative   brilliant   obviate
appropriate   comedian   piano
appropriation   create   radiation
area   created   radiator
areas   creative   variation

▶ WORD BEGINNING *In-*

incapable   inclined   increase
incentive   include   increased
inch   included   increases
incident   includes   incurred
incidental   inclusive   indebted
incidentally   incomprehensible   indebtedness
inclement   incorporated   indeed

indemnity	inspiration	intended
infants	install	intends
infer	installation	intention
inferior	installed	intimate
inferred	installment	intimated
influence	instance	invariably
influences	instant	inventory
injured	instead	invest
injuries	instruct	invested
injury	instructed	investigate
inlaid	instruction	investigation
insert	instructive	investment
inserted	instructor	invite
insertion	instrument	invited
inside	insurance	invoice
insist	insure	invoiced
insisted	insured	invoices
inspection	intend	involved

▶ **WORD BEGINNING** *Un-*

uncertain	unduly	unless
uncompromising	unfair	unloaded
uncontrollable	unfilled	unpacked
undecided	uninsured	unpaid
undoubtedly	unjust	unreasonable

unsatisfactory ⟋ℓ   unsettled ⟋⟍   until ⟑

▶ **WORD BEGINNING** *Unn-*

unknown ⟋⟍   unnecessary ⟋⟍ℓ   unnoticed ⟋⟍ℓ

▶ **WORD BEGINNING** *En-*

encountered ⟋⟍   engagement ⟋⟍   enjoyed

encourage ⟋⟍   engine   enjoyment

encouragement ⟋⟍   engineer   enlarge ⟋⟍

encroachment ⟋⟍   engineers   enrolled

endeavor ⟋⟍   engrave   en route ⟋⟍

engage ⟋⟍   engraver ⟋⟍   enthusiasm ⟋⟍

engaged ⟋⟍   enjoy   enthusiastic ⟋⟍

▶ **PHRASES**

we insist ⟋⟍   we invite ⟋⟍   you intend ⟋⟍

we intend ⟋⟍   who intend ⟋⟍   your intention ⟋⟍

Lesson 27

▶ **BRIEF FORMS**

idea	particulars	speak
ideas	probable	speaker
newspaper	probably	speaks
particular	regular	street
particularly	regularly	streets

subject 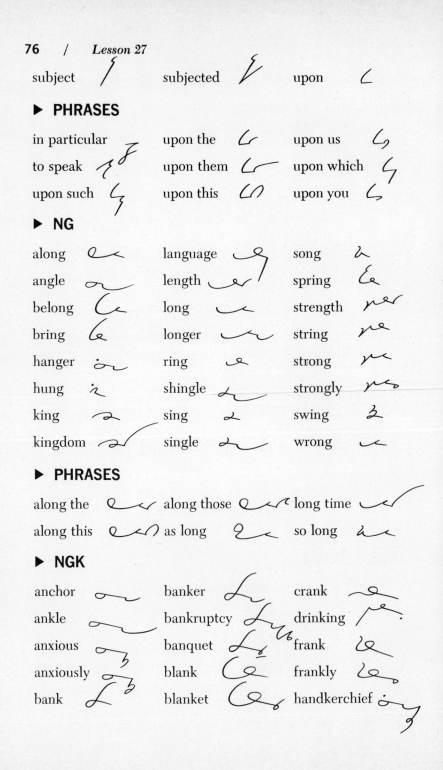   subjected   upon

▶ **PHRASES**

in particular   upon the   upon us

to speak   upon them   upon which

upon such   upon this   upon you

▶ **NG**

along   language   song

angle   length   spring

belong   long   strength

bring   longer   string

hanger   ring   strong

hung   shingle   strongly

king   sing   swing

kingdom   single   wrong

▶ **PHRASES**

along the   along those   long time

along this   as long   so long

▶ **NGK**

anchor   banker   crank

ankle   bankruptcy   drinking

anxious   banquet   frank

anxiously   blank   frankly

bank   blanket   handkerchief

ink	sanction	tank
link	shrinkage	tanker
pink	sink	uncle

▶ -TITION, -TATION, ETC.

accommodation	confirmation	permission
addition	consolidation	petition
additional	donation	quotation
admission	edition	recitation
combination	estimation	recommendation
commendation	foundation	repetition
commission	hesitation	reputation
commissioner	invitation	station
competition	notation	stationed
condition	omission	stationery

Lesson 28

▶ AH, AW

ahead	awaiting	awarded
await	awake	aware
awaited	award	away

▶ Y

yacht	yard	yarn

yarns	yellow	yoke
yeast	yes	young
yell	yield	youth

▶ X

affix	fixes	perplexing
appendix	flax	tax
approximate	flexible	taxed
box	index	taxes
boxed	indexes	taxation
boxes	maximum	taxicab
fix	mix	text
fixed	mixer	textile

▶ OMISSION OF SHORT Ŭ

Before n

apron	fun	run
begun	fund	runner
blunder	fundamental	runs
bunch	gallon	second
bundles	gun	secondary
comparison	lunch	son
country	luncheon	sun
done	punch	ton
front	refund	tonnage

Before m

become	lump	somewhere
bumper	plumbing	sum
column	some	summary
come	somebody	summer
drum	something	summons
income	sometime	vacuum
lumber	sometimes	welcome

Before a downstroke

among	flush	rushed
brush	functions	rushing
brushed	judge	tongue
budget	judgment	touch
clutch	junction	touched
conjunction	much	trunk
crushed	rush	trunks

▶ PHRASES

among the	being done	has done
among them	can be done	have done
among these	cannot be done	how much
among those	can't be done	I come
as much	could be done	I have done
be done	has come	must be done

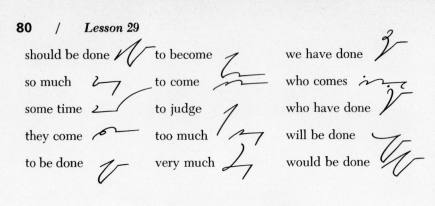

should be done	to become	we have done
so much	to come	who comes
some time	to judge	who have done
they come	too much	will be done
to be done	very much	would be done

Lesson 29

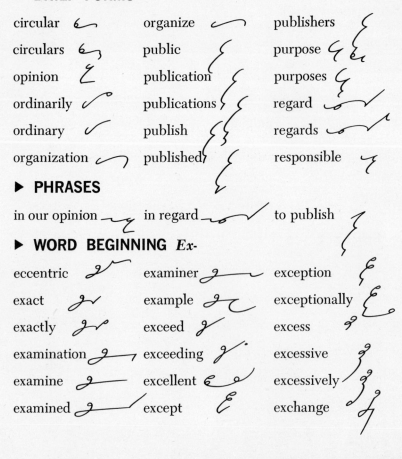

▶ **BRIEF FORMS**

circular	organize	publishers
circulars	public	purpose
opinion	publication	purposes
ordinarily	publications	regard
ordinary	publish	regards
organization	published	responsible

▶ **PHRASES**

in our opinion   in regard   to publish

▶ **WORD BEGINNING** *Ex-*

eccentric	examiner	exception
exact	example	exceptionally
exactly	exceed	excess
examination	exceeding	excessive
examine	excellent	excessively
examined	except	exchange

excited	expected	exposition
exclude	expects	express
exclusive	expedite	expressed
excuse	expend	expression
excuses	expended	extend
executed	expense	extended
executive	expenses	extends
exemption	expensive	extension
exhaust	experiment	extensive
exhausted	experimental	extensively
exhibit	expert	extent
exhibited	expiration	exterior
exhibition	expire	extra
exist	expired	extraordinary
existed	expires	extras
existence	explain	extreme
exists	explained	extremely
expansion	explains	inexcusable
expect	explanation	inexpensive

▶ **MD, MT**

ashamed	emptied	framed
claimed	empty	fumed
confirmed	exempt	gummed
deemed	famed	jammed

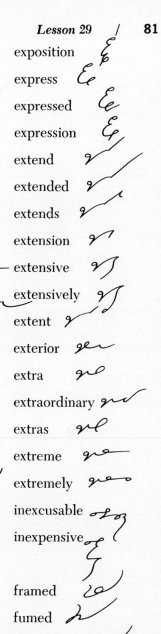

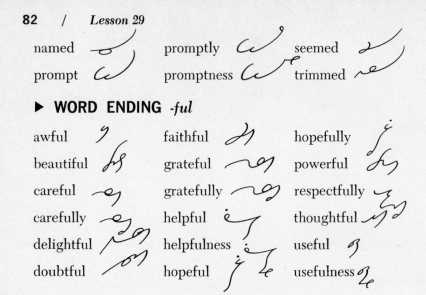

named

prompt

promptly

promptness

seemed

trimmed

▶ **WORD ENDING** *-ful*

awful

beautiful

careful

carefully

delightful

doubtful

faithful

grateful

gratefully

helpful

helpfulness

hopeful

hopefully

powerful

respectfully

thoughtful

useful

usefulness

Chapter
6

Lesson 31

▶ **BRIEF FORMS**

between	never	shortage
experience	nevertheless	shortages
experienced	quantities	shorten
experiences	quantity	shorter
inexperienced	recognize	shortest
merchandise	recognized	shortly
merchant	short	situation

▶ **PHRASES**

between the	between this	between us
between these	between those	between your

▶ **WORD ENDING** *-ure*

century	future	moisture
expenditure	lecture	natural
failure	literature	naturally
feature	mature	nature
fixtures	miniature	pasture

picture 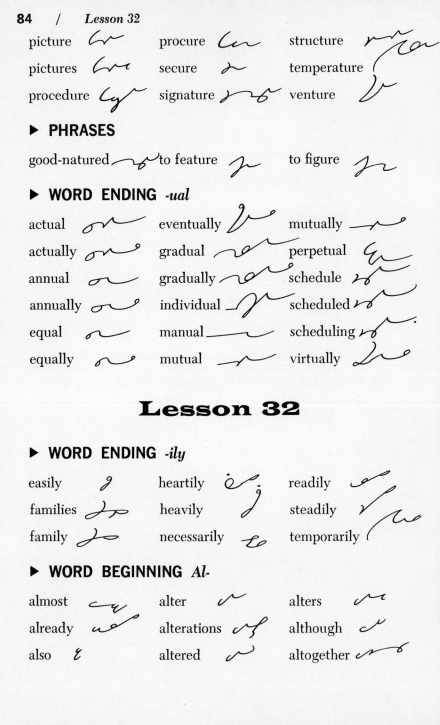   procure   structure

pictures   secure   temperature

procedure   signature   venture

▶ PHRASES

good-natured   to feature   to figure

▶ WORD ENDING -ual

actual   eventually   mutually

actually   gradual   perpetual

annual   gradually   schedule

annually   individual   scheduled

equal   manual   scheduling

equally   mutual   virtually

Lesson 32

▶ WORD ENDING -ily

easily   heartily   readily

families   heavily   steadily

family   necessarily   temporarily

▶ WORD BEGINNING Al-

almost   alter   alters

already   alterations   although

also   altered   altogether

▶ **WORD BEGINNING** *Mis-*

miscarry ____ misplaced ____ misunderstanding ____

mislaid ____ mistake ____ misunderstood ____

misleading ____ mistaken ____ mystery ____

▶ **WORD BEGINNING** *Dis-*

disappoint ____ discrepancy ____ dispatch ____

disastrous ____ discretion ____ display ____

disbursed ____ discrimination ____ disposal ____

disclose ____ discuss ____ dispose ____

discontinue ____ discussed ____ disposed ____

discontinued ____ discussion ____ disposition ____

discount ____ disinclination ____ dispute ____

discounted ____ dislike ____ dissolved ____

discouraged ____ dismiss ____ distance ____

discovered ____ dismissal ____ district ____

▶ **WORD BEGINNING** *Des-*

describe ____ despite ____ destiny ____

description ____ destination ____ destroy ____

descriptive ____ destined ____ destroyed ____

▶ **PHRASES**

he discussed ____ I described ____ I discussed ____

Lesson 33

▶ **BRIEF FORMS**

character	government	railroad
characters	object	railroads
govern	objection	throughout
governed	objective	world

▶ **PHRASES**

business world   throughout the   to govern

▶ **WORD BEGINNINGS** *For-, Fore-*

afford	forerunner	forth
effort	forget	fortune
efforts	forgive	fourth
force	form	inform
forced	formal	information
foreclosure	former	informed
foreman	formerly	misfortune
foremen	forms	unfortunate

▶ **WORD BEGINNING** *Fur-*

furlough	furnish	furniture
furnace	furnished	further
furnaces	furnishing	furthermore

▶ **PHRASES**

inform us   inform you   informing us

set forth    to forego   to form

setting forth   to forfeit   to furnish

to force   to forget   to perform

▶ *Ago* **IN PHRASES**

about ten days ago   long ago   some time ago

centuries ago   months ago   some years ago

few days ago   several days ago   weeks ago

few months ago   several months ago   years ago

Lesson 34

▶ *Want* **IN PHRASES**

he wanted   if you want   who want

he wants   they want   who wanted

I want   we want   you want

I wanted   we wanted   you wanted

▶ **ORT**

assorted   headquarters   quarter

assortment   mortal   quarterly

court   port   report

deportment   portable   reported

export   ports   reports

exportation   quart   resort

sort	sport	support
sorted	sports	supports

▶ OMISSION OF *R*

alternate	modern	term
alternative	northern	termed
attorney	northwestern	terminal
determine	pattern	terminate
determined	return	terms
eastern	returned	thermometer
eternal	southeastern	turn
external	southern	turned
fraternity	southwestern	western

▶ PHRASES

he returns	I returned	in return
he turned	I turned	to turn

▶ WORD ENDINGS *-cal, -cle*

analytical	historical	medical
article	identical	musical
automatically	identically	particle
chemical	logical	physical
chemicals	logically	political
critical	mechanical	practical
geographical	mechanically	practically

radical	surgical	typical
statistical	technical	typographical

Lesson 35

▶ **WORD BEGINNING** *Inter-*

interest	interim	interpreted
interested	interior	interrupted
interesting	intermediate	interruption
interests	internal	interval
interfere	international	interview
interference	interpretation	

▶ **WORD BEGINNING** *Intr-*

introduce	introduced	introduction

▶ **WORD BEGINNINGS** *Enter-, Entr-*

enter	enterprise	entrance
entered	entertain	entrances
entering	entertainment	unenterprising

▶ **WORD ENDING** *-ings*

bearings	clippings	feelings
beginnings	drawings	furnishings
buildings	earnings	hearings
casings	evenings	holdings

linings	openings	proceedings
meetings	paintings	savings
offerings	pleadings	servings

▶ PHRASES

Friday mornings	so many things
in this morning's	such things
many things	this morning's

▶ WORDS OMITTED IN PHRASES

at a loss	glad to see
at a time	I am of the opinion
at such a time	in a few days
bill of sale	in a few months
by the way	in a position
during the last	in addition to the
during the past	in addition to this
for a few days	in order to be
for a few minutes	in order to become
for a long time	in relation to the
for a minute	in such a manner
for a moment	in the future
glad to have	in the past
glad to know	in the world
glad to say	line of business

line of goods		out of the	
many of the		out of the question	
many of them		out of them	
men and women		out of this	
none of the		some of our	
none of them		some of the	
on the subject		some of them	
one of our		some of these	
one of the		some of this	
one of the best		some of those	
one of the most		son-in-law	
one of them		such a thing	
one of these		two or three	
one of those		up and down	
one or two		up to date	
ought to have		we are of the opinion	
out of date		week or two	
out of that		will you please	

Chapter 7

Lesson 37

▶ **WORD ENDING** *-ingly*

accordingly   exceedingly   seemingly

approvingly   increasingly   unknowingly

▶ **WORD BEGINNING** *Im-*

impairment	imposed	imprinted
impartial	impossible	imprinting
imperative	impracticable	improper
implements	impress	improved
import	impressed	improvement
imported	impression	reimburse
imports	imprint	reimbursement

▶ **WORD BEGINNING** *Imm-*

immoderate   immodest   immoral

▶ **WORD BEGINNING** *Em-*

embarrass	emphasis	employed
embarrassment	emphatically	employees
embraces	empire	employment

▶ OMISSION OF MINOR VOWEL

auditorium	millions	serious
companion	miscellaneous	seriously
courteous	period	situated
erroneous	periodical	theories
genuine	periodically	theory
graduate	previous	union
graduation	previously	valuation
ideal	radius	various

Lesson 38

▶ WORD ENDING *-ship*

fellowship	membership	scholarship
hardship	ownership	steamship
kinship	relationship	township

▶ WORD BEGINNING *Sub-*

subchief	submit	substance
subdivision	submitted	substantial
subeditor	subordinate	substantially
subhead	subscribe	substantiate
sublet	subscriber	subtracted
submission	subscription	subway

▶ JOINING HOOK AND CIRCLE VOWELS

drawee		poets		radios	
poems		portfolio		rayon	
poetry		radio		snowy	

Lesson 39

▶ WORD ENDING *-rity*

authorities		majority		securities	
charity		maturity		security	
clarity		prosperity		surety	

▶ WORD ENDING *-lity*

ability		inability		possibilities	
advisability		liabilities		qualities	
disability		locality		reliability	
facilities		nobility		responsibility	
facility		personality		sensibilities	

▶ WORD ENDING *-lty*

casualty		loyalty		royalties	
faculty		penalty		royalty	

▶ WORD ENDINGS *-self, -selves*

herself		itself		oneself	
himself		myself		ourselves	

themselves ⌢⁊   yourself ⫯   yourselves ⫯

► **PHRASES**

for itself ⫧   for themselves ⟋⁊   in itself ⟋

for myself ∠⌀   for yourself ⫯   of ourselves ⌁

for ourselves ∠⸲   for yourselves ⫯   with themselves ⌁⁊

Lesson 40

► **ABBREVIATING PRINCIPLE**

-tribute, -tribution

attribute ⌁   contribution ⌁   distribution ⌁

contribute ⌁   distribute ⌁   distributors ⌁

contributed ⌁   distributed ⌁   retribution ⌁

-quent

consequently ⌁   eloquent ⌁   frequently ⌁

delinquent ⌁   frequent ⌁   subsequent ⌁

-quire

acquire ⌁   inquire ⌁   require ⌁

acquirement ⌁   inquiries ⌁   required ⌁

esquire ⌁   inquiry ⌁   requirements ⌁

-titute, -titution

constitute ⌁   institution ⌁   substitute ⌁

institute ⌁   restitution ⌁   substitution ⌁

-titude

aptitude   fortitude   latitude

attitude   gratitude

-ology

apologies   biology   psychology

apologize   physiology   technology

apology   psychological   terminology

-itis

appendicitis   neuritis   tonsillitis

-ntic

Atlantic   authentic   frantic

-iety

propriety   society   variety

Lesson 41

▶ ABBREVIATING PRINCIPLE (*Concluded*)

algebra   convenient   inconvenienced

alphabet   conveniently   inconvenient

alphabetical   curriculum   memoranda

arithmetic   equivalent   memorandum

convenience   inconvenience   memorandums

philosophy ⟋   privileged   reluctance

privilege   privileges   reluctant

▶ WORD BEGINNING *Trans-*

transact   transfers   transmit

transaction   transit   transmittal

transcribe   transition   transmitted

transcript   translated   transparent

transfer   translation   transportation

transferred   transmission   transposition

▶ WORD ENDING *-ification*

classification   modification   ratification

identification   notification   specifications

justification   qualifications   verification

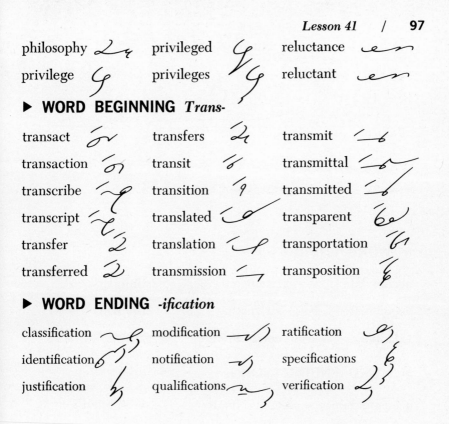

Chapter
8

Lesson 43

▶ **WORD ENDING** *-ulate*

accumulate   circulated   stimulate

accumulated   circulating   stimulated

calculate   congratulate   stimulates

▶ **WORD ENDING** *-ulation*

accumulation   congratulations   speculation

circulation   population   tabulation

▶ **WORD BEGINNING** *Post-*

postage	posthaste	postpaid
postal	postmark	postpone
postcard	postmaster	postponed
postdate	post office	postscript

▶ **WORD BEGINNING** *Super-*

superb	superintendent	supervision
superficially	superior	supervisor

Lesson 44

▶ **WORD ENDING** *-sume*

assume	consumer	presumed
assumed	consumes	presumptive
assumes	consuming	resume
consume	presumably	resumed
consumed	presume	resumes

▶ **WORD ENDING** *-sumption*

assumption	consumption	presumptions
assumptions	presumption	resumption

▶ **WORD BEGINNING** *Self-*

self-contained	self-made	self-satisfied
self-defense	self-pity	self-styled
self-educated	self-sacrifice	self-supporting

▶ **WORD BEGINNING** *Circum-*

circumstance	circumstances	circumvent

Lesson 45

▶ **WORD ENDING** *-hood*

boyhood	hardihood	neighborhood
childhood	manhood	parenthood

▶ **WORD ENDING** *-ward*

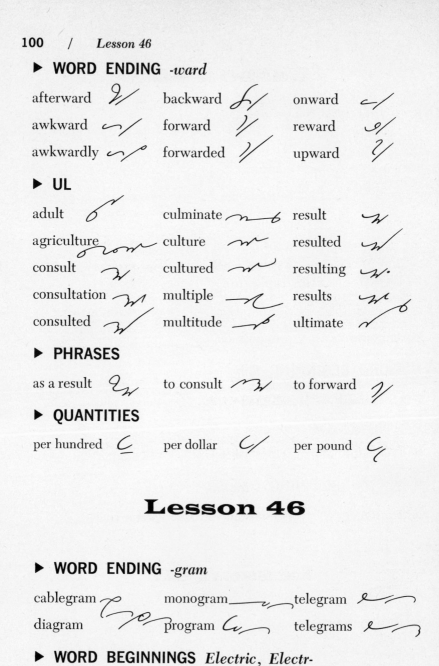

afterward   backward   onward

awkward   forward   reward

awkwardly   forwarded   upward

▶ **UL**

adult   culminate   result

agriculture   culture   resulted

consult   cultured   resulting

consultation   multiple   results

consulted   multitude   ultimate

▶ **PHRASES**

as a result   to consult   to forward

▶ **QUANTITIES**

per hundred   per dollar   per pound

Lesson 46

▶ **WORD ENDING** *-gram*

cablegram   monogram   telegram

diagram   program   telegrams

▶ **WORD BEGINNINGS** *Electric, Electr-*

electric   electrical   electrically

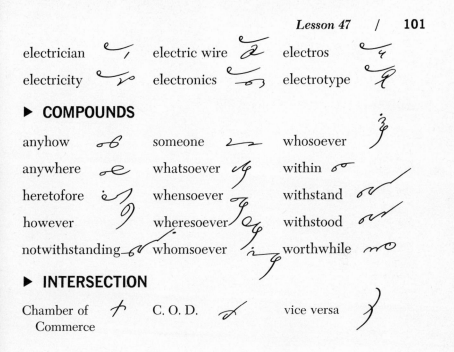

electrician	electric wire	electros
electricity	electronics	electrotype

▶ COMPOUNDS

anyhow	someone	whosoever
anywhere	whatsoever	within
heretofore	whensoever	withstand
however	wheresoever	withstood
notwithstanding	whomsoever	worthwhile

▶ INTERSECTION

Chamber of Commerce	C. O. D.	vice versa

Lesson 47

▶ GEOGRAPHICAL TERMINATIONS

-burg

Fitchburg	Harrisburg	Pittsburgh
Greensburg	Newburgh	Plattsburg

-ingham

Buckingham	Cunningham	Framingham

-ington

Arlington	Burlington	Irvington
Bloomington	Huntington	Lexington

Torrington *(shorthand)* Washington *(shorthand)* Wilmington *(shorthand)*

-ville

Brownsville *(shorthand)* Gainesville *(shorthand)* Louisville *(shorthand)*

Coatesville *(shorthand)* Jacksonville *(shorthand)* Nashville *(shorthand)*

Evansville *(shorthand)* Knoxville *(shorthand)* Zanesville *(shorthand)*

▶ **PHRASES**

Chicago, Illinois *(shorthand)* San Francisco, California *(shorthand)*

New York, New York *(shorthand)* St. Louis, Missouri *(shorthand)*

Appendix

The 500 most-used words presented in the order of their frequency in the Horn-Peterson "The Vocabulary of Business Letters."

1. I	17. be	33. my
2. the	18. are	34. had
3. and	19. not	35. our
4. to	20. as	36. from
5. a	21. order	37. am
6. you	22. at	38. one
7. of	23. this	39. time
8. in	24. with	40. he
9. we	25. but	41. received
10. for	26. on	42. get
11. it	27. if	43. please
12. that	28. all	44. do
13. is	29. so	45. been
14. your	30. me	46. letter
15. have	31. was	47. can
16. will	32. very	48. would

103

49. she

50. when

51. about

52. they

53. any

54. which

55. some

56. has

57. attention

58. matter

59. or

60. there

61. send

62. kindly

63. us

64. good

65. account

66. know

67. just

68. make

69. by

70. up

71. day

72. much

73. copy

74. made

75. same

76. out

77. her

78. also

79. yours

80. now

81. well

82. an

83. here

84. find

85. sent

86. them

87. glad

88. shipment

89. return

90. see

91. information

92. price

93. check

94. give

95. amount

96. advise

97. go

98. receipt

99. what

100. enclosed

101. note

102. come

103. were

104. credit

105. no

106. thank

107. how

108. herewith

109. however

110. other

111. wish

112. did

113. say

114. him

115. take

116. date

117. possible

118. his

119. got

120. work

121. over
122. number
123. may
124. company
125. present
126. before
127. hope
128. business
129. sending
130. only
131. being
132. two
133. balance
134. after
135. appreciate
136. regarding
137. service
138. more
139. first
140. could
141. enclosing
142. reply
143. interest
144. shall

145. receive
146. today
147. too
148. office
149. must
150. satisfactory
151. should
152. returned
153. like
154. year
155. their
156. covering
157. pleased
158. favor
159. stock
160. thanking
161. who
162. necessary
163. believe
164. department
165. line
166. therefore
167. cannot
168. forward

169. making
170. new
171. payment
172. sir
173. future
174. material
175. book
176. days
177. able
178. best
179. let
180. cover
181. trust
182. state
183. prices
184. feel
185. soon
186. further
187. next
188. through
189. above
190. bill
191. case
192. last

193. again
194. statement
195. care
196. think
197. each
198. upon
199. thing
200. list
201. want
202. given
203. way
204. part
205. kind
206. regard
207. returning
208. reference
209. hand
210. call
211. request
212. these
213. such
214. special
215. remittance
216. mail

217. three
218. fact
219. use
220. write
221. course
222. goods
223. size
224. hear
225. few
226. pleasure
227. desire
228. right
229. following
230. unable
231. past
232. referring
233. shipped
234. until
235. every
236. without
237. prompt
238. taken
239. month
240. week

241. old
242. cost
243. report
244. charge
245. writing
246. paid
247. orders
248. little
249. invoice
250. furnish
251. remain
252. might
253. once
254. yet
255. another
256. put
257. interested
258. replying
259. since
260. expect
261. records
262. man
263. place
264. back

265. promptly	289. better	313. under
266. delay	290. giving	314. several
267. understand	291. supply	315. big
268. money	292. contract	316. both
269. sorry	293. general	317. value
270. bank	294. its	318. acknowledge
271. opportunity	295. within	319. own
272. than	296. city	320. change
273. ordered	297. small	321. file
274. whether	298. accept	322. offer
275. complete	299. having	323. item
276. attached	300. during	324. pay
277. recent	301. many	325. freight
278. regret	302. position	326. advance
279. used	303. subject	327. name
280. sure	304. direct	328. try
281. school	305. always	329. advised
282. car	306. sale	330. dated
283. connection	307. ago	331. boy
284. sales	308. need	332. forwarded
285. enclose	309. full	333. items
286. going	310. reason	334. bad
287. books	311. ask	335. placed
288. because	312. off	336. separate

337. against
338. anything
339. great
340. greatly
341. written
342. claim
343. entirely
344. high
345. look
346. short
347. instructions
348. requested
349. additional
350. early
351. done
352. still
353. convenience
354. doubt
355. called
356. open
357. show
358. express
359. wrote
360. correct

361. condition
362. notice
363. years
364. merchandise
365. copies
366. long
367. original
368. large
369. bring
370. sample
371. catalogue
372. enough
373. careful
374. while
375. wire
376. already
377. ship
378. people
379. into
380. either
381. most
382. does
383. suggest
384. delivery

385. keep
386. second
387. assure
388. immediate
389. later
390. probably
391. bed
392. found
393. getting
394. duplicate
395. lot
396. seems
397. rate
398. consider
399. paper
400. refer
401. error
402. discount
403. shipping
404. indeed
405. collection
406. less
407. together
408. customer

409. gentlemen
410. consideration
411. inquiry
412. address
413. answer
414. asked
415. recently
416. appreciated
417. men _____
418. question
419. form
420. purchase
421. doing
422. charged
423. trusting
424. certainly
425. oblige
426. proper
427. writer
428. asking
429. sell
430. taking
431. total
432. why

433. record
434. showing
435. help
436. nothing
437. action
438. charges
439. settlement
440. expense
441. accordance
442. along
443. near
444. policy
445. unless
446. mind
447. correspondence
448. quite
449. rather
450. card
451. factory
452. far
453. calling
454. meet
455. weeks
456. sold

457. matters
458. reach
459. letters
460. particular
461. approval
462. meeting
463. stated
464. truly
465. dozen
466. close
467. saw
468. referred
469. class
470. page
471. although
472. months _____
473. relative
474. memorandum
475. addressed
476. arrange
477. handle
478. between
479. regular
480. cash

481. personal
482. trouble
483. coming
484. point
485. different
486. entire
487. issue

488. morning
489. house
490. draft
491. advertising
492. earliest
493. hold
494. cases

495. handling
496. secure
497. something
498. basis
499. wishes
500. certain

Index to Words

(Note: *a, 3* means that the word may first be written in Lesson 3, in *Gregg Shorthand, Diamond Jubilee Series.*)